FAST
FLOWERS

FAST
FLOWERS

JANE PACKER

DORLING KINDERSLEY LTD
London • New York • Sydney • Moscow
www.dk.com

A DORLING KINDERSLEY BOOK

www.dk.com

Project Editor
Annabel Kantaria

Art Editor
Emy Manby

Senior Art Editor
Tracey Clarke

Managing Editors
Susannah Marriott, Mary Ling

Managing Art Editor
Toni Kay

DTP Designer
Karen Ruane

Production Manager
Maryann Webster

Photography
Dave King

For Gary, Rebs, Lola and Ted
x

First published in Great Britain in 1998
by Dorling Kindersley Limited,
9 Henrietta Street, London WC2E 8PS

Copyright © 1998 Dorling Kindersley Limited, London
Text copyright © 1998 Jane Packer

4 6 8 10 9 7 5 3

A CIP catalogue record for this book is available
from the British library.

ISBN: 0 7513 0322 4

Reproduced in Italy by GRB Editrice, Verona
Printed and bound in Singapore.

CONTENTS

INTRODUCTION

THIS BOOK IS FOR the thousands of people who every so often buy a bunch of flowers, be it as they tear around the supermarket, rush home after a busy day, or suddenly feel inspired to visit their local florist. In other words, this book is not necessarily aimed at flower arrangers (in fact, mention the words "flower arranging" to many and they will beat a hasty retreat). My ideas are for all those who simply love flowers, but who perhaps don't have the time or inclination to plan and create the formal displays so beloved by ardent floral experts.

Not everyone wants to spend hours designing elaborate masterpieces (few of us have the time), but, with a little help, that bunch of flowers you have brought home and placed gingerly in the nearest vase can be transformed into an eye-catching arrangement.

This book will demonstrate that a few fast, slick ideas are all you need to be able to present your flowers successfully and with the minimum amount of fuss. Today's flower fashion is instant and spontaneous. It is a new look that suits modern lifestyles, and it bears scant resemblance to the complicated flower fantasies that are often on offer from designer florists.

Flowers should not be the preserve of specialists: their fragrance and colour lift every setting, and a simple, unconstrained display of blooms can evoke a sense of calm, create a mood of indulgence, and even seem to enhance our quality of life. The fast ideas that fill this book prove that all you need is a love of flowers and a little imagination to create a look that perfectly suits your modern lifestyle – enjoy!

Jane Packer

A GALLERY OF FLOWERS

THE GALLERY OF FLOWERS SHOWS JUST A FRACTION OF THE VAST

SPECTRUM OF VARIETIES AVAILABLE. SOMETIMES

THE COLOUR AND SHAPE OF A FLOWER IS

IMPORTANT FOR YOUR CHOSEN

LOOK, YET ONLY AN EXPERT

SUPPLIER COULD MATCH YOUR

DESCRIPTION TO A PARTICULAR

VARIETY. HOWEVER, THIS DELIGHTFUL

SELECTION WILL PROVIDE YOU WITH A RICH

STARTER PALETTE OF COLOURS, SHAPES AND

FRAGRANCES TO HELP YOU PLAN YOUR DISPLAYS.

KEY TO SYMBOLS

Lifespan: Short 🌷 Medium 🌷🌷 Long-lasting 🌷🌷🌷
Fragrance: Light ❀ Medium ❀❀ Strong ❀❀❀

NARCISSUS

THESE CHEERFUL SPRING FLOWERS can be identified by the characteristic trumpet or cup surrounded by a ring of six petals. Narcissus are cultivated in all shades of yellow, from the most delicate cream to deepest gold. The flowers are often sold without their foliage: expose long, straight stems as the deliberate focal point of a display. Mass narcissus together for a riot of yellows or mix them with other spring flowers for a bright splash of colour.

KEY FACTS

AVAILABILITY: Winter to spring
FRAGRANCE: ❀ ❀
LIFESPAN: 🌱 🌱

See also: Narcissus Topiary Tree 38; Instant Effects with Narcissus 40.

HYACINTHS & FREESIAS

THE HYACINTH'S DENSE SPIKE OF GLOSSY FLOWERS is heavily perfumed: choose from tones of lilac, pink, white and, more unusually, shades of apricot. Popular for wired bridal work, this spring bulb can also be used potted or in cut-flower arrangements. The trumpet-shaped freesia lasts well and its fresh colours and heady scent make it, too, a favourite at weddings. Mix and match bright shades or opt for the striking look of a single-colour bunch for an extra-special, fast display.

KEY FACTS: HYACINTHS	KEY FACTS: FREESIAS
AVAILABILITY: Winter to spring	AVAILABILITY: Winter to spring
FRAGRANCE: ❀ ❀ ❀	FRAGRANCE: ❀ ❀ ❀
LIFESPAN: ⚘ ⚘ ⚘	LIFESPAN: ⚘ ⚘

See also: Hanging Freesias 42; Hyacinth Centrepiece 44; Hyacinth Displays 46.

TULIPS

EVER-GRACEFUL AND HUGELY VERSATILE, tulips are cultivated in a rich variety of colours, shapes and sizes. More unusual examples include ornate parrot tulips with serrated edges, and double blooms with extra layers of petals. When using tulips in formal arrangements, be aware that once placed in water, all varieties will grow about 5cm (2in), and the heads will incline toward the light. Always look for a strong, firm leaf as a sign of quality.

KEY FACTS

AVAILABILITY: Winter to spring
FRAGRANCE: 🌸
LIFESPAN: 🕯 🕯

See also: Tulips in Raffia 48; Instant Effects with Tulips 50.

RANUNCULUS

WITH THEIR DENSE TIERS OF PETALS, these opulent flowers are reminiscent of ladies' ball gowns, looking their best when open and "full-skirted": sometimes, the fragile stems look as if they cannot support the weight of the petals.

The wide variety of colours available makes ranunculus versatile: en masse they can look very modern, or placed in a rustic jug and mixed with other flowers they take on a charming cottagey look.

KEY FACTS

AVAILABILITY: Late spring and autumn

FRAGRANCE: 🌸

LIFESPAN: 🌱 🌱

See also: White Ranunculus 52; Ranunculus Displays 54.

PEONIES

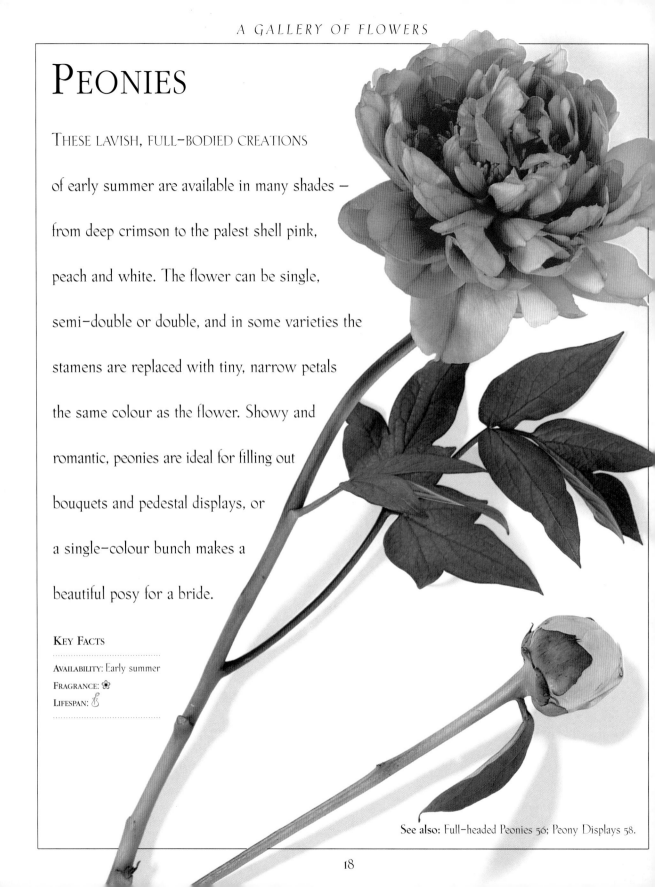

THESE LAVISH, FULL-BODIED CREATIONS

of early summer are available in many shades –

from deep crimson to the palest shell pink,

peach and white. The flower can be single,

semi-double or double, and in some varieties the

stamens are replaced with tiny, narrow petals

the same colour as the flower. Showy and

romantic, peonies are ideal for filling out

bouquets and pedestal displays, or

a single-colour bunch makes a

beautiful posy for a bride.

KEY FACTS

AVAILABILITY: Early summer
FRAGRANCE: ❁
LIFESPAN: ✿

See also: Full-headed Peonies 56; Peony Displays 58.

ROSES

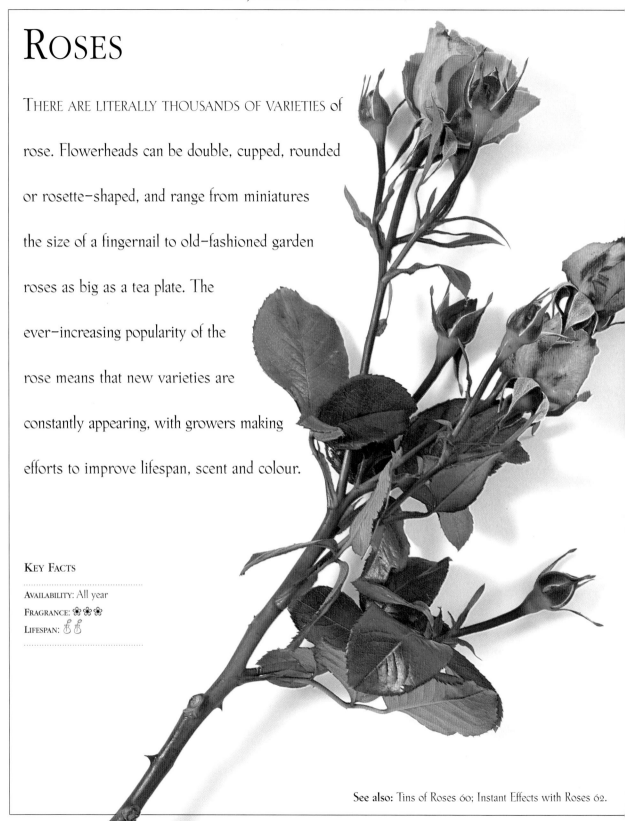

THERE ARE LITERALLY THOUSANDS OF VARIETIES of rose. Flowerheads can be double, cupped, rounded or rosette-shaped, and range from miniatures the size of a fingernail to old-fashioned garden roses as big as a tea plate. The ever-increasing popularity of the rose means that new varieties are constantly appearing, with growers making efforts to improve lifespan, scent and colour.

KEY FACTS

AVAILABILITY: All year
FRAGRANCE: ❀ ❀ ❀
LIFESPAN: ♀ ♀

See also: Tins of Roses 60; Instant Effects with Roses 62.

DIANTHUS

CARNATIONS, PINKS AND SWEET WILLIAMS are all part of the Dianthus family. There are hundreds of varieties of beautifully scented carnations and pinks, some showing patterned, rippled or serrated petals. Sweet williams grow in white or many shades of pink, from deep magenta to the palest rose pink. It is easy to transform carnations into fanciful arrangements, while pinks and sweet williams evoke dreamy thoughts of country gardens.

CARNATIONS

AVAILABILITY: All year
FRAGRANCE:
LIFESPAN:

PINKS/SWEET WILLIAMS

AVAILABILITY: Summer
FRAGRANCE:
LIFESPAN:

See also: Carnation Pots 64; Dianthus Displays 66.

SUNFLOWERS

NAMED FOR THEIR GLORIOUS YELLOW FLOWERS,

these floral giants are the epitome of hot summer days.

As cut flowers, however, they are available nearly all year,

and breeding has led to a range of novel characteristics

such as miniature heads, double rings of petals,

yellow centres and even amber petals.

KEY FACTS

AVAILABILITY: All year

FRAGRANCE: ❀

LIFESPAN: ♗

See also: Modern Sunflowers 68; Sunflower Displays 70.

DAHLIAS

DAHLIAS ARE AVAILABLE in varying sizes, with flowerheads

that include shapes such as pompon, waterlily, decorative and

cactus. The naive shape of the flower, along with a characteristic

palette of bright colours, has led to them being much imitated as

artificial flowers, despite being easy to grow in the garden.

Thanks to their versatility, dahlias need not be mixed

with other flowers – they can

look conventional in

a stoneware or enamel

jug, or modern in

a zany plastic vase.

KEY FACTS

AVAILABILITY: Late summer

FRAGRANCE: None

LIFESPAN:

See also: Fruity Dahlias 72;
Dahlia Displays 74.

LILIES

EXOTIC-LOOKING, SHOWY, COLOURFUL and often

fragrant, lilies are an excellent choice for cut-flower

displays. The white lily has a supreme grace that

makes it a favourite on special occasions.

Flowers are bowl, funnel,

Turk's cap or trumpet-shaped,

with petals sometimes striped

or dotted. Some florists

remove the stamens,

which can make

stubborn pollen

stains on fabric.

KEY FACTS

AVAILABILITY: All year
FRAGRANCE: ✿ ✿ ✿
LIFESPAN: 🪴 🪴 🪴

See also: Oriental Lilies 76; Lily Displays 78.

GERBERAS

THESE POPULAR, DAISY-LIKE FLOWERS are cultivated in an

ever-increasing array of varieties, including single, double

and fancy flowerheads with colours ranging from very

pale to bright and zingy. The simple shape

of the flower always seems modern and

perhaps even architectural, allowing

a single stem to steal the show in

a clear glass vase, or a few

well-chosen blooms to

update a more traditional

arrangement.

KEY FACTS

AVAILABILITY: All year
FRAGRANCE: None
LIFESPAN:

See also: Inside-out Gerberas 80; Instant Effects with Gerberas 82.

FRUIT & VEGETABLES

MANY ORDINARY FRUIT AND VEGETABLES make welcome additions to flower arrangements.

Although you can experiment with exotic items, the effects can be just as dramatic using

more easily obtainable ones. Colour counts, of course, when choosing produce, but the

most noticeable feature is often the skin – look for unusual texture or a radiant sheen.

CABBAGE LEAF VASE
Tie cabbage leaves around a
vase and fill with vegetables
and flowers that pick out the
wintry, purple tones.

See also: Fruity Dahlias 72;
Watermelon Vase 84.

RED APPLE

BLACK GRAPES

MINIATURE
PINEAPPLE

COURGETTES

AUBERGINES

SPRING ONIONS

RED ONION

CHILLIES

RADICCHIO

FOLIAGE

THE IMPORTANCE OF FOLIAGE in an arrangement should not be underestimated – the shape, colour and texture of the leaves can drastically alter the appearance of a flower. For example, stiff, upright, glossy foliage will make a rose look exclusive and elegant, but trailing foliage will make it appear more soft and feminine. Where possible, try to use seasonal foliage to complement seasonal flowers.

HYPERICUM

See also: Ivy Wreath 86.

Ruscus

Box

Leatherleaf

Spring Catkins

Berried Ivy

Laurustinus

Holly

Trailing Ivy

Eucalyptus

FIVE-MINUTE DISPLAYS

THIS SECTION SHOWS HOW TO ACHIEVE A POLISHED, COHESIVE LOOK IN A

MATTER OF MINUTES: ALTHOUGH SOME OF THE DISPLAYS MAY TAKE A LITTLE

LONGER, THEY ARE WORTH THE EXTRA EFFORT. BUT DON'T FEEL

BOUND TO COPY THESE IDEAS EXACTLY. INSTEAD, USE THEM

AS A SPRINGBOARD FOR YOUR OWN CREATIVE

COMBINATIONS AND REMEMBER TO CHOOSE

THE CONTAINER WITH CARE: SHAPE, SIZE AND

COLOUR ALL INFLUENCE THE END RESULT.

AS I HAVE SHOWN ON THE FOLLOWING

PAGES, EVEN THE SIMPLEST DESIGN CONCEPTS

CAN HAVE TREMENDOUS VISUAL IMPACT.

NARCISSUS TOPIARY TREE

YOU WILL NEED

Raffia

| 5–6 bunches of narcissus | Glass jar | Large terracotta pot | 2 handfuls of moss |

NOTHING LOOKS FRESHER for spring than a densely packed bundle of bright yellow narcissus. Rather than displaying the flowers in a vase, I have used them to make this unusual version of a topiary tree, contrasting the signature colour of the petals with a strong, dark container. The result is quirky, fun and very easy to make, but remember to top up the water to prolong the life of the flowers.

MAKING THE TOPIARY TREE

To keep the trunk of the topiary tree neat, make sure that the stems do not get twisted as they are put into position.

CREATE A DOME EFFECT with the heads by adding each circle of flowers lower than the previous one

1 Starting with one stem in your hand, add stems one by one in circles around it, positioning them so the heads face outward. After adding the last flower, tie raffia around the bunch, just below the heads, then trim the stems.

2 Place the tied stems in the glass jar half-filled with water, then position the jar in the terracotta pot. Press moss around the stems at the top of the pot to finish. Top up with water as required.

RAFFIA tied in a knot or bow

STANDING STEMS
Bound together, the bare, straight stems of the narcissus become the trunk of the topiary tree.

MOSS fills the gap between the stems and the vase

INSTANT EFFECTS WITH NARCISSUS

YOU CAN CREATE WILDLY DIFFERENT LOOKS with the variety of narcissus available, gaining as much impact from a single stem as from a large bunch massed together. Use other foliage to prevent the long narcissus stems from looking bare and choose a container carefully.

USING COLOUR AND SHAPE

INFORMAL TOPIARY
Choose a vase to emphasize the golden colour at the centre of each flower.

MASSED FLOWERS
Contrast pale flowers with a strong vase for a dynamic look.

COUNTRY LOOK
Use a vase in the same lime–green shade as the foliage to exaggerate its hue.

MODERN SIMPLICITY
Cut two varieties of blooms down short and pack into a contrasting blue glass vase.

COMPLEMENTARY COLOURS
Here, the foliage links the flowers with the vase, softening the look of the narcissus.

SIMPLE STEMS
Two stems of delicate flowers are perfect for the colour and shape of this bud vase.

PLANTED NARCISSUS
Use natural accessories, such as moss, stones and twigs, to dress up potted plants.

TWIG FENCING tied with green string links the colours of the basket and the stems

MOSS hides the potting soil

WIRE BASKET is a modern alternative to a wicker basket

HANGING FREESIAS

YOU WILL NEED

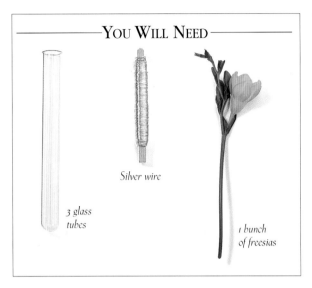

Silver wire

3 glass tubes

1 bunch of freesias

THE VIBRANT AND CHEERFUL COLOURS of freesias can be shown off to best advantage in the simplest displays. Here, dainty glass tubes containing a couple of stems are hung from gleaming silver wire. It is a versatile idea – you could pin a few to a pinboard to brighten up an office, hang several tubes across a window to catch the light, or tie single tubes to a tree for a novel Christmas decoration.

MAKING THE FREESIA DISPLAY

Make sure you have enough wire to hang the tubes at the desired height.

1 Wind the wire around the top of a glass tube to make a cuff, then twist to secure it.

2 Fill the tube with water and place one or two freesia stems in it. To finish, pin the tube to a pinboard, or hang it in a window.

FREESIAS have foliage-free stems that are ideal for this display

PINNED FLOWERS
A few of these fragrant arrangements fastened to a pinboard are a cost-effective way to bring colour to a room. Try to position them near a window to let the water and silver wire catch the light.

HYACINTH CENTREPIECE

YOU WILL NEED

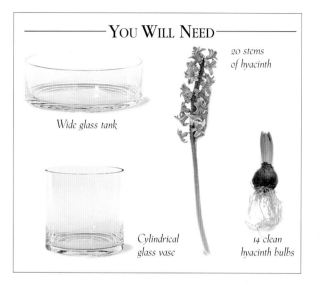

Wide glass tank

Cylindrical glass vase

20 stems of hyacinth

14 clean hyacinth bulbs

VERSATILE HYACINTHS are currently enjoying a revival as a fashionable flower. Change the mood of this magnificent display by experimenting with different containers: earthenware for a rustic country feel, glass for stark modernism. Here, the glass tank leaves the naked silver roots visible as they trail in the shimmering water, while the crown of deep purple bulbs makes the arrangement all the more tantalizing.

MAKING THE CENTREPIECE

Rest the bulbs on the edge of the glass tank, just above the water level. The cut flowers will last about 10 days, but change the water every 2–3 days.

1 Fill the vase with water and place it in the centre of the tank. Half fill the tank with water. Working from the outside in, arrange the cut hyacinths in the vase, slanting the stems neatly.

2 Place the bulbs, one by one, in a ring around the inner vase. Rest them on the rim of the tank so the roots touch the water, but make sure the bulbs themselves stay out of the water.

ADAPTABLE DISPLAY
When the cut flowers in the
centre begin to wilt, remove
them and fill the vase
with pebbles.

HYACINTH DISPLAYS

THE EARTHY TONES of terracotta pots are the perfect foil for the vibrant greens, pinks and purples of these hyacinths. A glass container filled with pebbles and shells creates a completely different look, while the loosely wrapped flowers would make a perfect simple gift.

CUT FLOWERS
Pay attention to the colour of the container: here, shocking pink and electric blue make the most of two simple arrangements.

BRIGHT TISSUE PAPER
tied with green string envelops a bunch of purple flowers

BLUE GLASS TUMBLER
gives easy charm to two stems of hyacinth

POTTED PLANTS
Make a refreshing change from cut flowers by planting hyacinth bulbs in shaped terracotta pots. Hide the soil with moss and remember to water regularly.

THE HYACINTH'S SPIKE of flowers adds a fresh scent to a room

BUDS are about to open

MOSS covers the soil and softens the overall effect

PEBBLES AND SHELLS surround a hyacinth planted in a glass tank

TULIPS IN RAFFIA

—YOU WILL NEED—

Large glass tank

Small glass vase

Bundle of raffia

4 edged tulips

6 pink tulips

10 purple tulips

THIS LUXURIOUS DISPLAY of tulips sits cradled in a bushy nest of raffia, dramatically changing the appearance of a plain glass tank. Although I have used raffia in a color that complements the tulips, the display would look equally stunning in clashing oranges, reds, and pinks. For a more natural look, fill the tank with pebbles, shells, wool in neutral tones, or textured tissue paper.

MAKING THE DISPLAY

To prevent rot, remember to remove the lower leaves from the tulips before putting them in water. For a stark, modern look, remove the leaves completely.

1 Fill the small vase with water and place it in the center of the glass tank. Push the raffia into the gap between the two containers so it completely hides the inner vase. Arrange the raffia to look attractive.

2 Position the purple tulips in a ring around the outer edge of the vase so their heads hang comfortably over the edge of the large tank. To finish, arrange the pink and edged tulips into a loose ring inside the purple ones.

NATURAL LOOK
This charming display is
achieved by placing the tulips
loosely so they do not
appear too formal.

PALE TULIPS form a
contrasting circle in the
centre of the arrangement

OUTER TULIPS
soften the look
by draping gently
over the edge of
the tank

RAFFIA BETWEEN
the vase and tank
hides the stems

INSTANT EFFECTS WITH TULIPS

WHAT COULD BE QUICKER than plunging a handful of flowers into a vase?

The key is to consider colour and form when matching flowers to vases, and to be bold,

whether using just a few stems or mixing a mass of blooms with foliage.

USING COLOUR AND SHAPE

STRONG STATEMENT
A bold choice of a bright cerise vase
is a shocking match for pink tulips.

SOFT PASTEL SHADES
Enhance the tulips' lemony tinge by
blending them with a pale yellow vase.

CONTRASTING TONES
For a lively modern display, juxtapose
fiery orange tulips with a green vase.

FLARED VASE
Fill this vase with enough stems to arch
over the edge in a sweeping curve.

NARROW-NECKED VASE
This shaped neck requires only a small
number of tulips to fill the vase.

LOW, WIDE BOWL
Don't be afraid to cut down tulips
for a low, compact display.

TERRACOTTA VASE is
filled with glossy, berried
ivy and parrot tulips

NEW WAYS
WITH FOLIAGE
Break the rules by wrapping
ivy leaves *around* the vase
(far right). Secured with
copper wire, these leaves
create a welcome alternative
to the ubiquitous cube glass vase.
Cut tulips low, so the heads appear
just above the rim.

WHITE RANUNCULUS

Flared glass vase

White shells and pebbles

30 stems of ranunculus

THIS COOL AND AIRY DISPLAY is easy to achieve using the heavy-headed blooms of white ranunculus. Choose a vase that flares out at the top: with a large quantity of flowers the stems will drape opulently over the side. The white shells and pebbles that fill the vase are not only evocative of sunny days and sandy beaches, they complement the colour of the ranunculus and help raise and support the stems.

MAKING THE DISPLAY

Feed the ranunculus stems between the shells and pebbles. This allows you to position each stem exactly where it is needed.

2 Place the ranunculus in the vase, working in a ring around the edge. Gently push each stem into the shells and pebbles. To finish, add stems to the centre of the display.

1 Half fill the vase with shells and pebbles, pulling the more attractive ones to the front. Fill the vase with water.

FLOWERS extend
well beyond the
edge of the vase

POLISHED SHELLS
shimmer in the water

PALE AND INTERESTING
Cool whites make this the
perfect decoration for hot
summer days.

RANUNCULUS DISPLAYS

THE NATURAL BEAUTY OF RANUNCULUS is such that I feel they
need no extra adornment. As layer upon layer of voluptuous
petals open, the heads appear to get heavier, making the
delicate stems bend and twist, allowing the flowers
to droop lazily over the edge of the container.

PURE AND SIMPLE
Mass white ranunculus together
in small aluminium pots and place
them on a silver tray around
a chunky cream candle.

BUDS provide
colour contrast

FIERY BRIGHT

Start by positioning the flowers around the edge of the container, then build them up toward the centre, resting them on each other. The display would also work with blooms such as marigolds or asters.

TOPIARY TREE
of pink ranunculus
(see page 38)

GLASS TUBES
draw attention to
the beautiful stems

RANUNCULUS are cut
down low and mixed
with gaultheria berries

FULL-HEADED PEONIES

LUSCIOUS PEONIES, familiar as country garden flowers, take on a contemporary look when a single-colour bunch is placed in a brightly coloured vase. Although the display looks very natural, the heavy-headed blooms are held in position with a grid of sticky tape, while the flared neck of the vase makes it possible to create a full display without using a huge number of flowers.

— YOU WILL NEED —

Sticky tape

Flared vase

12 mid-pink peonies

3 dark pink peonies

4 pale pink peonies

MAKING THE DISPLAY

Leave the stems in the centre of the arrangement slightly longer than the outside ones to create a domed effect, or cut them all to the same height for a flat-topped display.

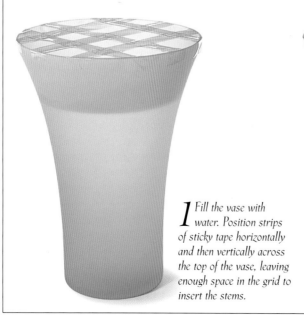

1 Fill the vase with water. Position strips of sticky tape horizontally and then vertically across the top of the vase, leaving enough space in the grid to insert the stems.

2 Starting from the outside, place one peony in each small corner hole of the grid, and two in each of the larger holes. Position them so the foliage surrounds the flowers.

CENTRAL BLOOMS are held
in place by a sticky–tape grid

YELLOW STAMENS
provide a delightful
colour contrast

OUTER RING of foliage
hides any visible sticky tape
and frames the flowers

FROSTED GREEN GLASS
vase gives the peonies
a modern feel

ONE COLOUR
A cluster of flowers in
the same shade sometimes
makes more of an impact
than a mixed bouquet.

PEONY DISPLAYS

THE LUSH OPULENCE OF PEONIES, their huge
heads crammed with masses of petals, makes
them one of my favourite flowers. Ideally
suited to an old-fashioned country look
when mixed with foliage and placed in
a jug, peonies can also look clean and
stylish in a contemporary glass vase.

RED CHERRIES
Position a tumbler of water
in the centre of the tank and
surround it with cherries.
Fill the tumbler
with peonies
and roses.

ZEBRA ROSES
work beautifully with
the peonies, adding
extra tones of pink

STEMS CUT TO DIFFERENT
heights give a natural look

COUNTRY GARDEN JUGS
To ensure your arrangement does
not look too contrived, group about
five stems of each flower together
within the display.

SPIKES OF PINK ASTILBE
blend with the pink peonies

LIME-GREEN
lady's mantle adds
vibrancy to the deep
pink of the peonies

ASTILBE FOLIAGE
frames the flowers

TINS OF ROSES

—YOU WILL NEED—

32 orange
roses

32 yellow
roses

4 watertight
tins

THIS CONTEMPORARY DISPLAY of roses plays with striking contrasts of colour and texture. The flowers are packed into square blocks of solid colour and any foliage that might interrupt the effect is stripped away. Cutting the stems short prolongs the life of the roses as water reaches the heads more easily. The look could also be achieved with other bold flowers such as tulips, anemones, carnations or asters.

MAKING THE DISPLAY

Make sure the roses are exactly the same height. If they differ even slightly, the impact of the blocks of colour will be lost.

1 Using one tin as a measure, cut the stem of the first rose at a sharp diagonal so the head sits just above the rim. Cut the rest of the roses to the same height. Fill the tins with water.

2 Line the edges of the tin with the tighter buds and use the more open flowers to fill the centre. Repeat this process using a single colour of rose in each tin. Arrange the tins.

CHEQUERED BED
Making four tins gives you
the flexibility to try different
arrangements: line the tins
up for a windowsill display
or push them together to
make a stunning focal point.

TIN CONTAINERS
contrast with the soft
ruffles of the flowers

FLOWERS support
each other

INSTANT EFFECTS WITH ROSES

INCREDIBLY VERSATILE and usually scented, roses have a fantastic ability to take on many different guises. Whether they look old-fashioned, romantic, modern or casual depends entirely on the vase you put them in, how you mix them with other flowers and which colours you choose.

USING COLOUR AND SHAPE

COLOUR SATURATION
Float a yellow rose in a yellow glass
container for dinner party elegance.

SYMPHONY IN WHITE
A pillar candle and white roses sit
well in a galvanized steel container.

TEST-TUBE DISPLAY
Stagger the height of the flowers for this
modern look, and do not fill every tube.

STEMS cut at
different heights
make the display
look casual

A FEW LEAVES
add colour contrast
to the display

"BOUDOIR" ROSES
Cut strong pink roses low and balance
them on the edge of a cream trophy
vase, cramming their heads together.

LONGER STEMS and larger heads are positioned in the centre of the arrangement

OUTER ROSES are arranged first, with their heads resting on the edge of the vase

METAL URN is not watertight, so it conceals a glass vase in which the roses are arranged

ENTRANCE HALL DISPLAY
This classical metal urn calls for a classical mix of blooms. I have used slightly open multi-coloured roses to give the impression of flowers just gathered from the garden.

CARNATION POTS

YOU WILL NEED

Painted
terracotta pot

Glass
tumbler

20
carnations

TRY TO RESIST THE URGE to place a bunch of carnations in a vase: instead, take a few moments to transform these flowers by cutting them short and massing them together. Accept that they will never tumble daintily over the edge of a vase, and work instead with their major features: straight stems and candy colours. Here I have emphasized their characteristic hues by painting terracotta pots in complementary shades.

MAKING THE DISPLAY

Use water-resistant oil paints to decorate the terracotta pots. It is an economical way to create vases in colours that will be suitable for your chosen flowers.

1 Fill the tumbler with water and place it inside the terracotta pot.

2 Place the carnations in the glass, cutting the stems so the heads rest in a ring around the edge of the pot. To finish, fill the centre with slightly longer stems.

HEADS PACKED CLOSELY
together give dense colour

TERRACOTTA POT
painted with water-
resistant oil paints

SEASONAL VARIATIONS
Try using different colours
to match the seasons – red
flowers in a green pot for
Christmas or orange flowers
in a brown pot for autumn.

DIANTHUS DISPLAYS

CONTRARY TO POPULAR BELIEF, carnations can look contemporary if you work with, rather than against, their sugary colours. Bound together and placed in painted terracotta pots, the long stems and full heads form impressive topiary trees. A moody bouquet shows off the drama of a dark variety, while a frothy, lilac arrangement brings sweet williams, pinks and hydrangeas bang up to date with a zingy painted pot.

BRIGHT RAFFIA
binds stems tightly
below the heads

SUMPTUOUS RED
ROSES add an
extravagant touch

ROMANTIC BOUQUET
Make a posy (see page 114) of
stunning dark red carnations, red
roses and striped sweet williams,
and tie it with pink raffia.

CARNATION TOPIARY TREES

The long, straight stems of
carnations are perfectly suited
to creating topiary trees. Add
the stems to your hand one
by one, bind them tightly
and place in a tumbler inside
a painted pot.

CARNATION HEADS
are massed together
for an intense burst
of colour

DELICATE PINKS
fill gaps between the
large hydrangea heads

PURPLE VASE

Paint a pot with a mix
of oil paints to give a
modern colour that
updates the old-fashioned
look of sweet williams,
pinks and hydrangeas.

MODERN SUNFLOWERS

I HAVE USED BRIGHT YELLOW RAFFIA to magnify the colour of these bold sunflowers and give this rustic look a modern twist. The height of the vase balances out the bushiness of the flowerheads, while the green foliage breaks up the yellow. When the flowers start to wilt, pull the petals off to reveal the green layer underneath, and use different coloured raffia or upholstery cord for a variation on the theme.

MAKING THE DISPLAY

Cut the stems so they are slightly taller than the vase. Leave the centre ones slightly longer. To prevent rotting, strip off the leaves that would lie below the water level.

1 Starting at the bottom, wind the raffia around the vase. When you come to the end of a length of raffia, tie the next length to it and continue. Completely cover the vase with raffia.

2 Fill the vase with water. Place the sunflowers in a ring around the edge of the vase, slanting the stems so the heads rest on the rim. To finish, fill the centre with slightly longer stems and use any spare leaves to fill gaps.

SUNFLOWER LEAVES
add a contrasting
colour to the display

RAFFIA hides the
clear glass vase,
giving it a very
different look

SUMMER SUN
Yellow raffia emphasizes the
sunny colour of the flowers,
but gold cord would make a
creative alternative.

SUNFLOWER DISPLAYS

WHEN USING SUNFLOWERS, it is too easy to let them take on their usual "country" look,
so here I have used earthenware vases in warm colours to give the display a Provençal flair.
In contrast, the three stems in modish glass tubes bring the arrangement up to date. When
the petals start to wilt, try pulling them off to reveal the green underlayer. Do not be afraid
to cut sunflowers down low – the single stem in the earthy, glazed pot is an example of how
even a tight budget can achieve a stunning display – sometimes less is definitely more.

BRONZE AND GOLD
Warm, sandy colours link these
jaunty wooden blocks with the
more traditional terracotta vases.

SUNFLOWERS with the
petals removed provide
a contrasting colour

GLASS TUBES in
wooden blocks
add modern style

DECORATED TERRACOTTA
gives a Mediterranean look,
perfect for sunflowers

SUNBURST
Working from the outside
in, place the sunflowers in
concentric circles. Rest the
heads of the outer flowers
on the edge of the vase.

FRUITY DAHLIAS

Coloured vase   *5 tangerines*   *9 dahlias with*
                       on sticks   *foliage*

IF YOU WANT AN INNOVATIVE NEW LOOK, why limit yourself to flowers? For this fun-filled arrangement, I decided that bright orange tangerines would make a perfect accompaniment for the wine-red pompon dahlias. The jaunty foliage stripped from the flowers breaks up the heavy colours and adds shape to the display, while a contemporary vase in tangy apricot emphasizes the dark petals of the dahlias.

MAKING THE DISPLAY

Use scissors to make a hole in each tangerine. Use the dahlia stems as sticks if they are strong enough, otherwise garden canes or other woody stems will do.

1 Fill the vase with water, then place the tangerines around the outer edge of the vase.

2 Add the dahlias between the fruit, filling gaps with foliage stripped from the flowers. To finish, place another ring of slightly taller dahlias and foliage in the centre.

CENTRAL DAHLIAS are slightly taller than the outer ones

TANGERINES are supported on the rim of the vase so they do not squash the flowers

FOLIAGE breaks up the round shapes of the flowers and tangerines

FRUIT AND FLOWERS
This arrangement would also work using apples, lemons or limes with matching flowers.

PLACE THE VASE on a low table so it can be viewed from above.

DAHLIA DISPLAYS

THE WIDE VARIETY OF COLOURS, shapes and sizes of dahlia makes it easy to create vibrant displays without introducing other types of flower. Here, the lime–green plastic bowl reflects the almost artificial brightness of the blooms, giving a vivid, modern look to flowers more often seen in the garden. To make this arrangement, cut the dahlias down low and mass their heads together for an intense burst of late–summer colour.

SIMPLE BUT SWEET
This display is proof that quantity is not everything. If you choose colours carefully, it is possible to make an impact without masses of flowers.

DARK RED DAHLIAS are set off by the lime–green bowl

GROUPS of the same colour flowers give more impact than single blooms

LEAVES fill out the bowl

INNER BLOOMS have
slightly longer stems
than outer ones

CLUSTERED FLOWERS
Rest the heads of the outer circle
of flowers on the rim of the bowl.
Then work from the outside in,
resting each concentric circle on
the previous one.

DAHLIAS spill over
the side of the bowl

FOLIAGE frames
the flowers

ORIENTAL LILIES

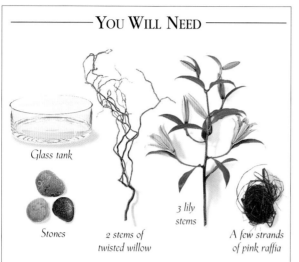

Glass tank

Stones

2 stems of
twisted willow

3 lily
stems

A few strands
of pink raffia

JUST A FEW LILY STEMS are needed to make this sculptured display, and look how it transforms the flowers. The look is modern and ethereal, hinting at oriental style. The display's great height and elegance call for it to be placed on a side table in a large, but simple, room. I prefer to keep the flowers pale and use bright raffia to add flashes of colour, but you could choose to highlight bold lilies with subtle raffia bows.

MAKING THE DISPLAY

Prepare the display in position as it is very heavy and awkward to lift once made. Top up the water every few days.

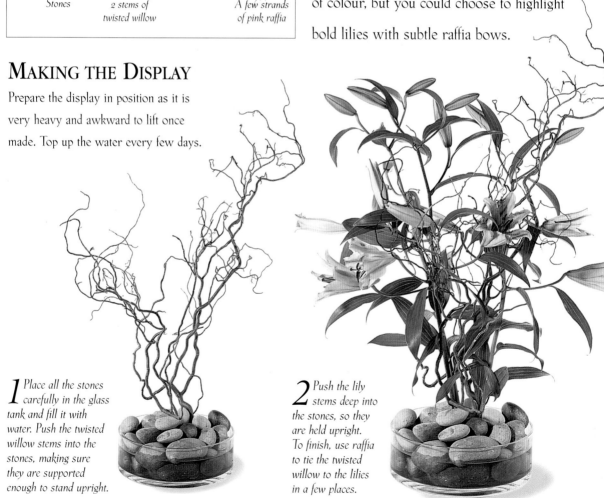

1 Place all the stones carefully in the glass tank and fill it with water. Push the twisted willow stems into the stones, making sure they are supported enough to stand upright.

2 Push the lily stems deep into the stones, so they are held upright. To finish, use raffia to tie the twisted willow to the lilies in a few places.

RAFFIA BOWS
complement the
colour of the lilies

STEMS are
supported by
the stones

WATER is deep enough
to reach the stems

MINIMAL STYLE
This sparse arrangement suits
a house decorated in a minimal
style. It would look fantastic in
an uncluttered, airy room.

LILY DISPLAYS

PURE AND ELEGANT, lilies demand simple containers to show
them at their best. Heavy-bottomed clear glass vases are
ideal: in a light room, where the sun catches the water,
the effect is dazzling. Choose vases that mirror and
complement the different shapes of the flowers – long
arum lilies look best in a tall, thin vase, while a single
white flower rests languidly on the rim of a low bowl.

DARK PINK
lilies clustered in
a square glass tank

FLOWERS AND FOLIAGE
drape over the edge
of the vase

CRYSTAL CLEAR
Enhance the sparkling effect of the
glass vases by placing a few together,
and change the water every day to
keep it looking fresh and clean.

DARK GREEN
monstera leaves
highlight the pink
of the oriental lilies

ARUM LILIES call for
a tall vase that supports
the graceful stems

STEMS ARE STRIPPED
of foliage to keep the
water clean

INSIDE-OUT GERBERAS

YOU WILL NEED

Glass tumbler

Rubber band

Stems cut from 10 gerberas

Yellow string

10 gerberas

OFTEN THE PERFECT VASE is not to hand when you need it, so I believe in raiding the kitchen for equipment. These gerberas are arranged in an ordinary drinking glass, which is hidden from view by a ring of crisp green stems tied in position with coloured string. Two or three of these simple arrangements, using different coloured flowers, would look perfect on a window ledge or as a table centrepiece for a casual lunch party.

MAKING THE DISPLAY

Cut the gerberas to the right height for the tumbler and save the stems for decoration. If your flowers do not have long enough stems, surround the tumbler with green beans instead.

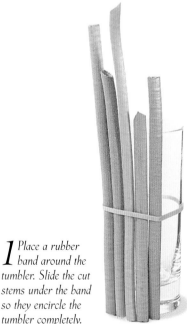

1 Place a rubber band around the tumbler. Slide the cut stems under the band so they encircle the tumbler completely.

2 Bind the stems in position with yellow string, then remove the rubber band. Cut the circle of stems to the height of the tumbler, fill it with water and arrange the flowers.

GERBERAS all cut to the
same height give the
impression of cramming

STRING tied in
a simple knot
adds charm and
colour contrast

THE "NO-VASE" SOLUTION
I first saw this method
used by the Parisian florist,
Christian Tortu. It works
equally well with almost any
long−stemmed flower such as
narcissus, anemones and lachenalia.

INSTANT EFFECTS WITH GERBERAS

WHEN USING GERBERAS, it is important to match your flowers to the vases you have at home. The myriad of colours available and the simple shape of the flowers mean a single stem can look stylish and modern, while abundant arrangements work well too.

USING COLOUR AND SHAPE

DOUBLE STRENGTH
Keep vase and flowers the same colour for maximum impact.

TWO COLOURS
Add a contrasting shade to bright yellow flowers in a yellow glass jar.

LONG-STEMMED GERBERA
Use bright green glass to highlight the purity and freshness of this white flower.

FIVE STEMS
Fill a narrow-necked vase with five stems that pick out the colour of the vase.

TEN STEMS
For a stronger arrangement, add five more stems in a complementary colour.

FIVE STEMS WITH FOLIAGE
One or two large leaves, such as these anthurium leaves, give instant drama.

FLOWERS at random
heights give the display
an informal look

GREEN STEMS without
foliage emphasize the
simplicity of the display

TERRACOTTA POT is not
watertight: it hides a glass jar in
which the gerberas are arranged

PERFECT PARTNERS
An ideal match of container and flowers:
the washed dots on the terracotta reflect
the pale colour of the gerberas, while
the scalloped edge of the pot echoes the
shape of the petals.

WATERMELON VASE

USING FRUIT TO MAKE A VASE gives the display originality. I have avoided filling this hollowed-out watermelon with a cocktail of tropical flowers, choosing instead to highlight the dusty grey-green tones of its skin with hydrangea and sea holly. Although too special for everyday use, this luscious arrangement could be a splendid feature at a buffet party, perhaps sitting alongside melons crammed with delicious finger food.

— YOU WILL NEED —

Ornamental cabbage

Watermelon

2 heads of hydrangea

1 stem of berried ivy

1 stem of sea holly

MAKING THE DISPLAY

If you choose a large melon you will need more flowers and foliage to fill the shell.

1 *Slice the top off the watermelon and scoop out the flesh. Fill the shell with water and place the ornamental cabbage at the front.*

2 *Add the hydrangea and ivy to the arrangement, working around the edge of the melon shell. To finish, place the sea holly in the centre.*

SEA HOLLY picks out the blue
tones of the cabbage leaves

THICK GREEN LEAVES
of the ornamental cabbage
make a dramatic centrepiece
for the display

CHANGING SEASONS
To adapt the look to suit the
changing seasons, you could
also use pumpkins, gourds,
marrows and cabbages.

IVY WREATH

YOU WILL NEED

String

5 branches of larch or twigs	5 branches of larch or twigs, sprayed gold	3 long strands of ivy, lightly gilded with gold spray paint	3m (3¼yd) of rope, sprayed gold

THE TRADITIONAL APPROACH to wreath–making requires time, patience, specialist equipment and expertise, but these simple wreaths, made from winter foliage, prove that original and modern looks can be achieved in a few minutes. The method adapts well to different styles – holly branches give the wreath a truly Christmassy feel, but bare twigs could be decorated with foliage and scented flowers for summer.

MAKING THE IVY WREATH

Choose only the freshest, most supple twigs and branches to make this wreath, or it will be difficult to bend them into a circle. Use gold spray paint to highlight leaves and branches for a more opulent effect.

1 One by one, twist the branches around each other to form a long, thick piece, binding with string if necessary. Bend into a circle and bind tightly. Squash the wreath into shape, snip off messy pieces and use them to fill gaps.

2 Wind the ivy in and around the wreath, positioning the gold leaves evenly throughout. To finish, cover the string by winding the gold rope around it, leaving a decorative strand of rope hanging down each side of the wreath.

GOLD ROPE is left hanging to give the wreath a contemporary elegance

FESTIVE FOLIAGE

The type of foliage you choose has a direct impact on the final look of the wreath. For a traditional Christmas look (above), team fresh branches of berried holly with a luxurious shot–silk ribbon in rich tones of red and green.

SPRING ARRANGEMENTS

SPRING FLOWERS need minimum fuss for maximum impact. The secret is to choose a
vessel that works with the flowers and the interior of your house, but remember that
a vase can dramatically alter the mood of a display. I have picked orange containers
to exaggerate the hues of the lachenalia and fritillaria, while galvanized buckets
give a more contemporary feel, particularly when arranged in a line
and teamed with flowers in glorious shades.

ALL IN A ROW
Purple muscari, green ivy and
bright primulas in miniature,
galvanized buckets create
cheerful bursts of colour.

SILVERY SENECIO
reflects the tone
of the container

SPRING
COLOURS
To create a group
of arrangements
that work well
together, balance
height and colour
when you choose
the containers.

FIERY JUG picks up
the warm hues of
the fritillaria

LACHENALIA drapes
gently over the side
of a coffee cup

89

SUMMER ARRANGEMENT

MASSES OF SUMMER FLOWERS are packed into this enamel tub to create a natural-looking display of summer abundance in the countryside. Although the flowers are placed randomly in the tub, they are grouped together by type, as if they were still growing in the garden. It is a versatile look that works with many types of flower; try mixing size and colour to achieve the look you want.

YELLOW MARIGOLDS add colour between the pink peonies and green lady's mantle

WHITE PLUME-LIKE
astilbe contrasts with the
lushness of peonies

WHITE ASTRANTIA
softens the clash of deep
blue cornflowers and
vivid orange marigolds

GARDEN BOUNTY
Group each type of flower into
a bunch, bind them, and cut the
stems flat. Fill the bath with
enough water to cover the
stems, then position the flowers.

AUTUMN ARRANGEMENT

THIS BOUNTIFUL DISPLAY OF BERRIES and fruit crammed into an earthy terracotta pot reflects the abundance of the autumn harvest. The wide-necked container gives the display a full, rounded shape, allowing branches and tendrils to drape decadently over the sides.

AUTUMNAL EUCALYPTUS contrasts with red of rosehips

FRESH APPLES are speared on potting sticks, then positioned

TERRACOTTA POT is the quintessential container for autumnal arrangements

COTONUS contrasts with
other autumn colours

BERRIED IVY is a patch of
green between hypericum
and spindle berries

HYDRANGEA flowers
are positioned with
heads hanging down
to look natural

HARVEST FESTIVAL
Place bundles of foliage
in a bucket inside the
terracotta pot, putting
the taller bundles at the
back and pointing bunches
in different directions.

WINTER ARRANGEMENTS

THESE SEASONAL DISPLAYS demonstrate the importance of co-ordinating vase colour with content. A vase can exaggerate and emphasize tones and shades, dramatically changing the impact of the flowers. Below, I have dusted variegated ivy with a hint of silver paint to reflect the frosted feel of the cast-iron container while, on the right, I have matched bright red berries and dark foliage with a red glass vase for festive winter warmth.

PROMINENT LEAVES are
highlighted with a hint
of silver spray paint

CAST-IRON CONTAINER
enhances the pale, frosted tones
of the flowers and foliage

SILVER AND WHITE
Randomly mass together
hyacinths, ranunculus,
Christmas roses, mistletoe,
eucalyptus and variegated
ivy dusted with silver paint.

VASE looks striking
when light shines
through the red glass

BERRY RED
A mixture of dark winter
foliage and berries tones
perfectly with a deep-red
glass vase: in another
container the effect would
be less dramatic.

SPECIAL EFFECTS

PARTIES AND SPECIAL OCCASIONS CALL FOR MORE THAN JUST A

BUNCH OF BLOOMS ON A SHELF OR WINDOWSILL – THEY PROVIDE

THE PERFECT EXCUSE FOR ADORNING YOUR HOME WITH CREATIVE

COMBINATIONS OF VIVID FLOWERS, VIBRANT GREEN FOLIAGE

AND MELLOW CANDLELIGHT.

OFTEN THE FOCAL POINT OF A ROOM, MANTELPIECES CAN

BECOME A STRIKING CENTREPOINT FOR A CELEBRATION, WHILE A FEW

SIMPLE FLOWERS AND SOME TRAILING FOLIAGE ON A DINING TABLE

CAN EFFECT A MAGICAL TRANSFORMATION FOR AN EVENING PARTY.

THE PAGES THAT FOLLOW FEATURE A SELECTION OF MY FAVOURITE

IDEAS FOR YOU TO ADAPT TO SUIT YOUR PERSONAL STYLE.

SUMMER TABLE DISPLAY

YOU WILL NEED

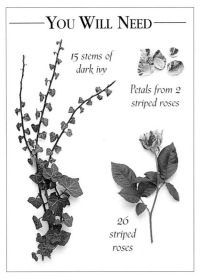

15 stems of
dark ivy

Petals from 2
striped roses

26
striped
roses

WHEN TIME IS OF THE ESSENCE, a table setting can be swiftly transformed by weaving trails of ivy and dappled rose heads among the plates, and scattering the display with fragrant rose petals. Napkins wound with a tendril of ivy and a single rose complete the romantic summer table. Deep red roses combine equally well with ivy for a sumptuous Christmas display.

MAKING THE DISPLAY

Trail ivy all around and over the edge of the table. Place the rose heads in clusters on the table and tuck rose leaves beneath them, then sprinkle petals on the tablecloth.

A SPRIG OF LEAVES lies
beneath the cut–down
rose stem

1 Tie a length of ivy loosely around a rolled napkin. Trim the ivy, making sure the ends are long enough to trail over the rim of a side plate.

2 Cut down a rose stem to about 10cm (4in) and remove the leaves. Tuck a sprig of leaves under the twist of ivy, then push in the rose.

TRAILS OF IVY create
long, flowing lines

PACIFIC-STYLE TABLE

YOU WILL NEED

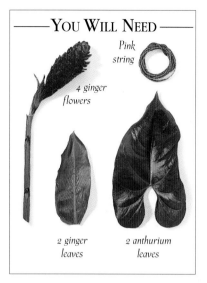

Pink
string

4 ginger
flowers

2 ginger
leaves

2 anthurium
leaves

BRING A SUGGESTION OF THE ORIENT to your dining room with this exotic table setting, which is based on clever use of striking colours. Set against an azure tablecloth, the lustrous pink flowers and dark, glossy leaves are fast and easy to arrange, yet sophisticated enough to impress even the most discerning dinner guests.

MAKING THE DISPLAY

Make sure the ginger leaves are supple enough to bend around the flower stems – if they are too dry they will crack.

FIVE PIECES OF STRING tied in
one knot add decorative detail

1 Strip any foliage from the ginger flowers and place two stems together. Wrap a ginger leaf around the stems.

2 Cut five lengths of pink string and use them all to tie the wrapped leaf in place. To finish, place in the centre of the table, on top of the anthurium leaves.

CHRISTMAS DINING TABLE

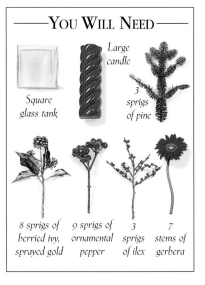

— YOU WILL NEED —

Square glass tank

Large candle

3 sprigs of pine

8 sprigs of berried ivy, sprayed gold

9 sprigs of ornamental pepper

3 sprigs of ilex

7 stems of gerbera

NO CHRISTMAS TABLE is complete without candles and flowers, yet who wants to spend the festive period hunting for specialist equipment? This simple candle and foliage display is quickly assembled and can be prepared at the last minute or a few days in advance. If you cannot find gerberas, choose other bold flowers in colours to complement your tableware.

MAKING THE DISPLAY

If you have time, expand the theme by lying a single bloom on each napkin and tying a name tag to each flower.

1 Place the candle in the centre of the glass tank and fill the tank with water. Position the pine sprigs around the candle, pointing them in different directions.

2 Add the berried ivy, ornamental peppers and ilex around the candle. Dot the gerberas around the centre to finish.

BEACHCOMBER MANTELPIECE

BLUES, GREENS AND GREYS, pebbles and rope: these bits and pieces look as if they have been gradually gathered from a blustery seaside and placed lovingly on this mantelpiece. Standing in simple glass tumblers, eucalyptus and cabbage continue the natural theme, while a hand-tied bundle of eucalyptus pods is propped casually behind the stone candle holders.

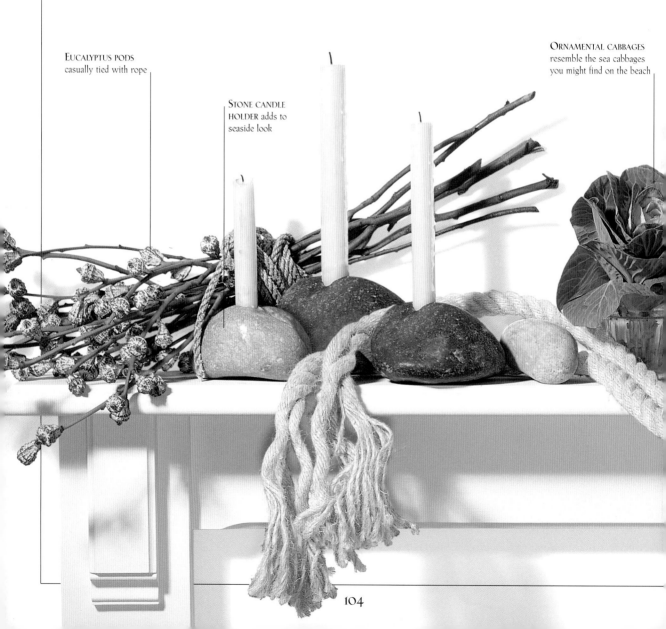

EUCALYPTUS PODS
casually tied with rope

STONE CANDLE
HOLDER adds to
seaside look

ORNAMENTAL CABBAGES
resemble the sea cabbages
you might find on the beach

SILVER-GREY TONES
of the eucalyptus pods add
to the beachcomber image

PEBBLES enhance
the colours of
the cabbages and
eucalyptus pods

ROPE ties the
display together

GERBERA MANTELPIECE

THE KEY TO THIS DISPLAY is its simplicity. Clear glass containers allow the long, curvy gerbera stems to become as much a feature of the display as the blooms, while the jelly–bean colours of these modest flowers make them a winning choice for a contemporary interior. Fewer stems, rather than more, keep the look uncluttered and bold. Other flowers with strong colours, large heads and bare stems, such as tulips, anemones and amaryllis, work in similar arrangements.

DIFFERENT AMOUNTS of water in each vase create an interesting visual effect

GERBERA stems are cut to varying lengths to give an impression of spontaneity

LONG BENDY STEMS are a feature of the display

TWO OR TEN
This display is just as stunning if you use only a few containers.

ANEMONE MANTELPIECE

REPETITION AND REGULARITY lie at the heart of this graphic arrangement: the anemones are equidistant and each laurel leaf hangs at exactly the same height. Wrap laurel leaves around glass tumblers and tie with wire, then fill the glasses with anemones, packing their heads together. Suspend extra laurel leaves from lengths of wire.

GLOSSY LEAVES
are hung at exactly
the same height ———

ANEMONES are cut
so the heads rest on the
rims of the tumblers

LAUREL LEAVES
wrapped around
the tumbler ————

SUSPENDING LEAVES
Twist the wire around the stem of each leaf, then hang the leaves above the mantelpiece.

ALTERNATIVE IDEA
If you cannot find laurel leaves, try making the display with fresh ivy leaves.

GOLDEN WIRE
ties the wrapped leaves in place

GREEN CANDELABRA

YOU WILL NEED

Candelabra

6 candles

15 baby's tears plants in 3 shades of green

1 large glass jar

16 glass jars

2 glass vases

IF YOU THINK A CANDELABRA is too elaborate for everyday use, try dressing it down with plants such as these delicate green baby's tears. I have used lime candles and green glass to emphasize the radiant colour of the leaves and to contrast with the hard silver colour of the metal. Use the candelabra as a dining table centrepiece, or remove the inner ring of plants, light the candles and hang it from the ceiling instead.

MAKING THE DISPLAY

Introduce more colour by filling some of the pots with cut flowers or candles in different shades.

1 Place the candelabra in position on the table. Remove the baby's tears from their pots and re-plant in the small glass jars. Place the plants in a few of the candelabra holders and in a ring around the inside of the candelabra.

2 Fill the remaining candelabra holders with plants and candles in jars and vases. To finish, put three candles in the large glass jar and place it in the centre of the ring.

HOOK allows candelabra to hang, if the arrangement is adapted accordingly

GLOW IN THE DARK
If you wish to use the candelabra at night, replace a few plants with extra candles to give more light.

CLUSTER OF CANDLES draws the eye to the centre of the candelabra

INNER RING of plants gives the impression of fullness

GIFT IDEAS

FLOWERS CAN MAKE A SUPERB LAST-MINUTE GIFT. IT TAKES

JUST A FEW FRESH IDEAS TO TURN A MODEST BUNCH OF

FLOWERS INTO A BEAUTIFUL BOUQUET OR GIFT

ARRANGEMENT. SOME OF THE FOLLOWING

SUGGESTIONS REQUIRE A LITTLE ADVANCE

PLANNING BUT, FOR THOSE OF YOU WANTING INSTANT

RESULTS, I HAVE INCLUDED IDEAS THAT WILL ENABLE

YOU TO TURN EVEN A HASTILY PREPARED GIFT INTO A

MINIATURE MASTERPIECE OF SIMPLE DESIGN.

BRIDAL POSY

YOU WILL NEED

50 stems of freesia | *String* | *White tulle, 3 x 1m (3¼ x 1yd)*

THE SWEET PERFUME OF FREESIAS makes them a perpetual favourite with brides. Update the candy–coloured freesia posy of the sixties by keeping to a single–colour bunch and using large–headed double freesias. This extravagant posy of luscious, creamy flowers becomes quite ethereal when swathed in masses of white tulle; white ribbon tied in a bow would give a more understated look, yet still be effective.

MAKING THE POSY

For an opulent posy, choose luxurious double freesias. Bind the stems tightly so the posy does not fall apart during the day.

STEMS placed at an angle make a spiral shape

1 Hold one stem in your hand, then build up the posy by adding stems one by one, each stem at slightly more of an angle than the last.

2 Use string to bind the flowers tightly just below the heads. Cut the stems level and to a length that is comfortable to hold in the hand.

3 *Cut a strip of tulle 30cm x 1m (12in x 1yd). Fold the remaining tulle in half lengthways and scrunch it up in both hands. Wrap it around the posy so the stems are covered. Use the cut strip to tie the tulle in place.*

PERFECT POSY
The white freesias and tulle make this ideal for a bride; use brighter flowers and a different fabric for a bridesmaid.

BOLD BOUQUETS

WITH A LITTLE IMAGINATION, bouquets can be made to suit practically any person and almost every situation, as these flamboyant and contemporary examples show. Swathes of ruffled tissue paper make the bouquets themselves look like huge exotic flowers – choose colours to complement or contrast with the blooms. Use the method for making posies, see page 114.

CRIMSON PAPER complements inky purple monkshoods, pink roses, arum lilies, eucalyptus and dark green foliage

CERISE TISSUE PAPER
encircles frothy hydrangeas
and lush roses in pink and red

GREEN CHRYSANTHEMUMS,
poppy heads, variegated
box, sedum and *Garrya
elliptica* are arranged around
anthuriums and wrapped in
lime–coloured tissue paper

GIFT-WRAPPED BOUQUET
For an extra–special wrapping
(see above), hold the flowers
upright in the centre of a
square of tissue paper.
Gather the paper up
around the stems
and tie just below
the heads.

PLANTED ORCHIDS

FOR A REALLY SPECIAL GIFT, these plants will outlast cut flowers every time. Always consider the recipient's surroundings and personality when making a gift, and look carefully at the flowers for help when choosing a container. The bleached colours and tropical blooms in this arrangement would suit a modern, airy environment; the size of the trug and height of the flowers make it ideal for a low table.

MAKING THE DISPLAY

Take the orchids out of the arrangement to water them; the display should last up to 4 weeks.

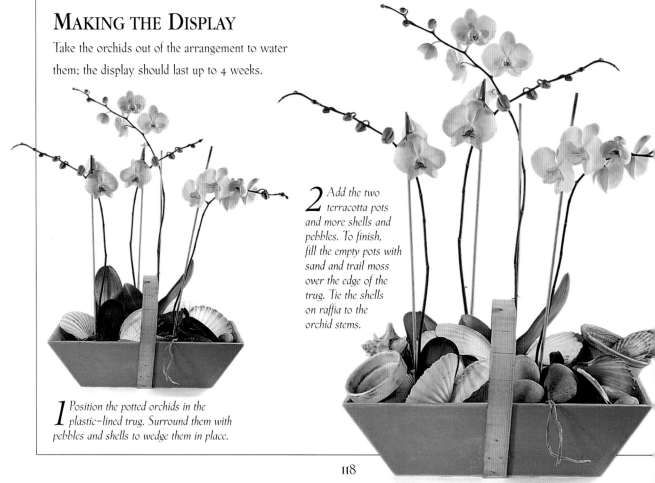

1 Position the potted orchids in the plastic-lined trug. Surround them with pebbles and shells to wedge them in place.

2 Add the two terracotta pots and more shells and pebbles. To finish, fill the empty pots with sand and trail moss over the edge of the trug. Tie the shells on raffia to the orchid stems.

IDEAL GIFT
This effective display
is surprisingly easy
to assemble and evokes
thoughts of sunny days.

RAFFIA
is decorated
with shells

ORCHID ROOTS
dangle over the
edge of the trug

VALENTINE HEART

YOU WILL NEED

8 dark
red roses

6 pink
roses

8 stems of
fuchsia

4 stems of
photinia

4 stems of
hypericum

Gold
string

2 x 2m (2¼ x 2¼yd)
of cellophane

Red tissue
paper

Heart-shaped
box

WHY NOT CELEBRATE VALENTINE'S DAY with a posy made from roses, the emblem of romance? This lush explosion of velvety pink and berry red fits snugly into a heart-shaped box to make a glamorous surprise for your loved one. Although roses are particularly sensitive to water deprivation, the cellophane wrapping holds enough water to sustain them until they can be transferred to a vase.

MAKING THE POSY

Cut the stems to a length that matches the depth of the box, allowing the lid to fit comfortably without damaging the heads of the flowers.

1 Make the posy (see page 114). Measure out enough cellophane to gather up around it and create a pouch. Place the posy in the centre of the cellophane.

2 Gather the cellophane around the posy and tie it carefully with string. Fill the bottom of the cellophane pouch with water by pouring it down through the middle of the posy. To finish, place the posy upright in the box.

PHOTINIA adds lightness to the display while continuing the red theme

A SINGLE ROSE is tied to the lid with gold cord

RED TISSUE PAPER lining the box adds drama to this sumptuous gift

VALENTINE GLAMOUR
The different tones of red and the delicate pink fuchsia give the impression of opulence and, ultimately, of romance.

WRAPPING GIFTS

BEFORE YOU REACH FOR BOWS AND RIBBONS, look how a well-chosen flower can transform an ordinary package. A silver box with two *Amaryllis belladonna* attached could contain an anniversary present, while the same box adorned with a single, triffid-like anthurium promises something exotic. Try raiding the garden for material: a hydrangea and some string can look frivolous yet fresh where a bow might look fussy.

FROTHY PINK HYDRANGEA is an attractive alternative to a bow

PINK RIBBON intertwined with *Amaryllis belladonna* adds feminine charm

A PEACH COLOURED
GERBERA complements
a lilac bag

BAGS OF STYLE
Floral decorations
are an easy way to
personalize gifts,
instantly giving them
a home-made look.

PURPLE PUFF-BALL
ALLIUMS peek out
of a gift bag

AN ANTHURIUM jazzes
up a striped ribbon

A SIMPLE ARUM LILY is
an elegant finishing touch

A LEUCOSPERMUM
tied with yellow string
hints at the exotic

TECHNIQUES & SKILLS

ANY FLOWER ARRANGEMENT, whatever the size, will last longer if you take a couple
of minutes to prepare the stems in advance. The basic techniques on these pages show how
to spiral stems to give your displays a good shape, and how to cut and clean stems
to encourage flowers to take up water. A method for straightening stems is also included
as this can strengthen flowers as well as make them look more healthy.

SPIRALLING STEMS

*1 Hold the first stem in one
hand, and add the next
at a diagonal angle. One by
one, add more stems, each
one at slightly more of an angle
than the previous one.*

*2 Continue adding the stems
in this manner, so they form
a spiral pattern. Use your thumb
to hold them in position.*

*3 When the bunch is complete,
cut the stems to the same length
and drop them into the vase, letting
them fall naturally into shape.*

PREPARING STEMS

1 Strip the stems of all foliage that will be below the waterline. This helps keep the water clean and looks neat and tidy.

2 Gently scrape each stem with a knife. This removes any thorns, bumps, and old plant tissue from the stems.

3 Cut the stems on a slant. This creates a larger surface area, which allows the stem to take up water more efficiently.

STRAIGHTENING STEMS

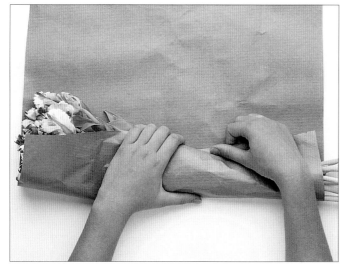

1 Straight flower stems give an arrangement extra height and make flowers that tend to wilt quickly, such as tulips, easier to display. To straighten bent stems, wrap them in brown paper and secure with tape or string.

2 Stand the wrapped stems in a deep container of warm, fresh water for a few hours, or overnight, until they straighten.

INDEX

Author's Acknowledgments

I would like to say a big thank you to my wonderful team
at my shops and school for all their help and support.

Thank you, too, to Annabel, Emy and Tracey for endless diligence
and help in producing this book and for always pushing things a
little further. A huge thank you to Dave King for his wonderful
photography, patience and help, and grateful thanks to June for those
fantastic lunches that saw us all through.

Publisher's Acknowledgments

Dorling Kindersley would like to thank Claudia Norris and
Rachana Devidayal for design assistance; Nasim Mawji, Lorna
Damms, Monica Chakraverty and David Summers for editorial
assistance; Stephen Einhorn for the stone candle holders on pages
104–5; Tony Cross and Pam Brinkhurst at Wilford Bulb Company;
Philip Tivey & Sons, growers of dahlias and other plants since
1956; John Mattock; David Root at Kelways Ltd; Langport, Somerset;
Bloms Bulbs Ltd, Bedford; the Flower Council of Holland.
Photography by Dave King except: Mark Hamilton 35, 94–5.
Index: Sue Bosanko